W9-BBX-392

DISCARD

VALLEY PARK
ELEMENTARY LIBRARY

The Wonder of
HAWKS

ANIMAL WONDERS •

ANIMAL WONDERS •

To Indra, Beatrice, Deneb, and Liila. May you always have a chance
to see a hawk in a bright fall sky! — Sumner Matteson

**For a free color catalog describing Gareth Stevens' list of high-quality books and
multimedia programs, call 1-800-542-2595 (USA) or 1-800-461-9120 (Canada).
Gareth Stevens Publishing's Fax: (414) 225-0377.
See our catalog, too, on the World Wide Web: http://gsinc.com**

Library of Congress Cataloging-in-Publication Data

Ritchie, Rita.
    The wonder of hawks / by Rita Ritchie and Sumner Matteson ; photographs by
John Hendrickson ; illustrations by John F. McGee.
        p. cm. — (Animal wonders)
      "Based on . . . Hawk magic for kids . . . by Sumner Matteson"—T.p. verso.
      Includes index.
      Summary: Text and photographs introduce members of the hawk family,
with emphasis on the Cooper's Hawk.
      ISBN 0-8368-1560-2 (lib. bdg.)
      1. Hawks—Juvenile literature. 2. Cooper's hawk—Juvenile literature.
[1. Hawks. 2. Cooper's hawk.] I. Matteson, Sumner W. II. Hendrickson, John, ill.
III. McGee, John F., ill. IV. Matteson, Sumner W. Hawks. V. Title. VI. Series.
QL696.F32R57   1996
598.9'16--dc20   96-4999

First published in North America in 1996 by
Gareth Stevens Publishing
1555 North RiverCenter Drive, Suite 201
Milwaukee, WI 53212 USA

This edition is based on the book *Hawk Magic for Kids* © 1995 by Sumner Matteson, first
published in the United States in 1995 by NorthWord Press, Inc., Minocqua, Wisconsin, and
published in a library edition by Gareth Stevens, Inc., in 1995. All photographs © 1995 by
John Hendrickson except front cover, pp. 7, 11, 21, 27, 28-29, 40-41, 44-45 © 1995 Tom Stack
and Associates, with illustrations by John F. McGee. Additional end matter © 1996 by
Gareth Stevens, Inc.

All rights to this edition reserved to Gareth Stevens, Inc. No part of this book may be reproduced,
stored in a retrieval system, or transmitted in any form or by any means, electronic, mechanical,
photocopying, recording, or otherwise without the prior written permission of the publisher except
for the inclusion of brief quotations in an acknowledged review.

Printed in the United States of America

1 2 3 4 5 6 7 8 9 99 98 97 96

80079

598.9
RIT

$ 13.46

The Wonder of
HAWKS

by Rita Ritchie and Sumner Matteson
Photographs by John Hendrickson
Illustrations by John F. McGee

Gareth Stevens Publishing
MILWAUKEE

4

Watching a Cooper's hawk catch a rabbit is an incredible sight. After the rabbit is caught, the hawk holds the prey in its sharp talons. It tears off pieces of meat with its hooked beak.

Cooper's hawks can be seen in North America all year. But some Cooper's hawks spend winter as far south as Costa Rica. The birds can be observed migrating in spring and fall.

A Cooper's hawk makes its nest in the *V* of a tree. The nest can be 40 feet (12 meters) above the ground. It is built with sticks.

Cooper's hawk

Newly hatched hawks are blind. But soon, they can see better than humans can. Hawks have two tiny pits, called fovea, at the back of each eye. These help hawks see clearly over long distances.

Cooper's hawk

Cooper's hawks usually build a new nest on top of an old one. But sometimes they use the same nest as the year before.

Northern goshawk

Each year, the female lays three to five eggs. The male brings food to the female as she sits on the nest. He sits on the eggs while she eats. The eggs hatch after thirty to thirty-six days.

VALLEY PARK
ELEMEN   LIBRARY

12

Cooper's hawk eggs hatch in June. The newborns are covered with white down. They can only lift their heads to take food.

Northern goshawks

Cooper's hawk (left)

The down soon
grows thicker.
Then the young
are able to
withstand some
rain and cold.
The parents can
leave them for
short periods. In
a few weeks, the
young are covered
with feathers.

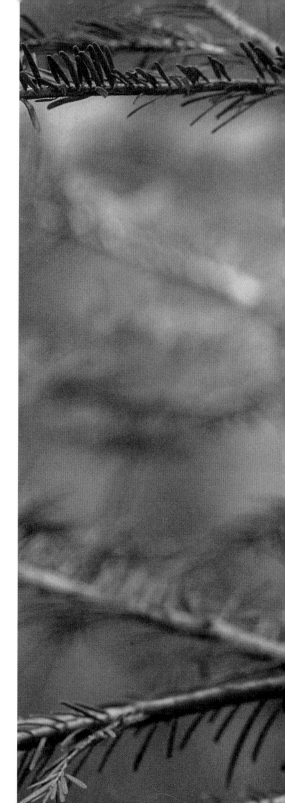

Sharp-shinned hawk

16

In fall, hawks migrate from areas in the north to escape the coming winter snows. Food is in short supply during winter in northern areas. The hawks search for warm air masses, called thermals, rising from the ground. These thermals help carry the hawks south.

Osprey

Red-tailed hawk

As they fly south, hawks join other hawks. They form large groups called kettles. When it rains or the wind shifts, the hawks rest in trees or on the ground until conditions are better.

Most hawks migrate during the day. Many people gather in certain areas to watch hawks migrate. Some types of hawks belong to a group of birds called accipiters.

Accipiters have long tails; long legs; and short, rounded wings. All hawks are carnivores, or meat-eaters. They eat small birds, snakes, lizards, and small mammals.

There are three kinds of accipiters in North America — the Cooper's hawk, the sharp-shinned hawk, and the northern goshawk.

Cooper's hawk

Sharp-shinned hawk   *Northern goshawk on next page*

When accipiters fly in an open sky, they flap their wings (five times usually) and glide. They do this again and again. Accipiters can also fly swiftly through a forest. They dodge right and left, and up and down very quickly.

When a Cooper's hawk gets near prey, it fans its wings to slow down. Then it swings its legs out (like the man in the picture), using sharp talons to grab the prey. Parent hawks feed their babies until six weeks after the young first take flight. Then the young can hunt on their own.

Osprey on next page

The fastest hawk
in the world is the
peregrine falcon.
It can fly faster
than 175 miles
(280 kilometers)
per hour! The
female peregrine
is about 12 inches
(30 centimeters) tall.
It has a wingspan of
about 3 feet (1 meter).
The male is smaller.

People
once
used a
chemical
called
DDT
on crops.
But
DDT was
harmful to
hawks and
other animals.
It caused hawks' eggs to crack,
and the peregrine nearly died
out completely.

Buteos form another group in the hawk family. Buteos have long, broad, rounded wings. They have short broad tails, and short legs and feet.

Red-tailed hawk

Buteos eat mice, frogs, snakes, lizards, birds, and turtles. The broad-winged hawk, the red-tailed hawk, and the Swainson's hawk are the best-known buteos.

Red-tailed hawks

41

In Wisconsin, red-tails begin nesting in late February.

Broad-wing hawks migrate thousands of miles from northern lands to Central and South America.

*Red-tailed hawks
on final pages*

When hawks
fly, they give us
a strong sense
of courage
and freedom.

Glossary

accipiter – a type of hawk that has a long tail; long legs; short, rounded wings; and low, zigzag flight

buteo – a type of hawk that has long, broad, rounded wings; a short, broad tail; short legs and feet; and soaring flight

carnivore – a plant or animal that eats meat

fovea – small pits inside the eye of a hawk that provide acute, or sharp, vision

kettles – large groups of hawks that form during migration

migrate – to move periodically from one region or climate to another for breeding or feeding

prey – an animal eaten by another animal for food

talons – the claws of a bird of prey

thermal – a rising mass of warm air

Index